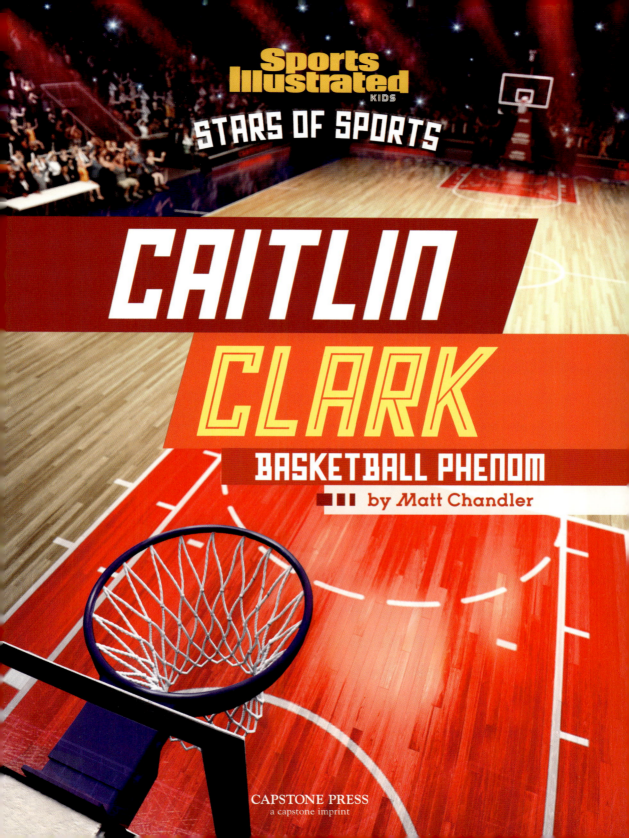

Published by Capstone Press, an imprint of Capstone
1710 Roe Crest Drive, North Mankato, Minnesota 56003
capstonepub.com

Copyright © 2025 by Capstone. All rights reserved. No part of this publication may be reproduced in whole or in part, or stored in a retrieval system, or transmitted in any form or by any means, electronic, mechanical, photocopying, recording, or otherwise, without written permission of the publisher.

SPORTS ILLUSTRATED KIDS is a trademark of ABG-SI LLC. Used with permission.

Library of Congress Cataloging-in-Publication Data is available on the Library of Congress website.
ISBN: 9798875219627 (hardcover)
ISBN: 9798875219634 (paperback)
ISBN: 9798875219641 (ebook PDF)

Summary: From her early days playing basketball in Iowa to her professional WNBA career with the Indiana Fever, learn all about Caitlin Clark and how she's changed women's basketball in this inspirational sports biography.

Editorial Credits
Editor: Christianne Jones; Designer: Bobbie Nuytten; Media Researcher: Svetlana Zhurkin; Production Specialist: Katy LaVigne

Image Credits
Alamy: Timothy Mulholland, 10; Associated Press: Cliff Jette, 17, Jessica Hill, 25; Getty Images: © 2024 NBAE/Bri Lewerke, 20, © 2024 NBAE/Ron Hoskins, 21, Carmen Mandato, 13, Chet White, 26, Elsa, 5, 19, Gregory Shamus, 7 (top), Joe Buglewicz, 23, 28, Kevin C. Cox, 8, Maddie Meyer, 11, Matthew Holst, 16, 27, NCAA Photos/Ben Solomon, 14, Sarah Stier, 18, Steph Chamber, cover, 15; Newscom: Icon Sportswire/Marc Piscotty, 9; Shutterstock: anek.soowannaphoom, 7 (bottom), Oleksii Sidorov, 1

Source Notes
Page 11, "I think playing for . . ." Adam Hensley, "Driven with Confidence: How Caitlin Clark Became a Hawkeye," si.com, April 22, 2020, https://www.si.com/college/iowa/basketball/caitlin-clark-042120, Accessed September 24, 2024.

Page 16, "I'm sad we lost this game . . ." March Madness, Iowa National Championship Postgame Press Conference, youtube.com/watch?v=NE6rI8Dkcvw, Accessed September 24, 2024.

Page 24, "It's a good little taste of what's possible . . ." Andrea Adelson, "Caitlin Clark's Record Year of Basketball Ends in Playoff Sweep," espn.com, September 26, 2024, https://www.espn.com/wnba/story/_/id/41447804/indiana-fever-star-caitlin-clark-record-year-basketball-ends-playoff-sweep, Accessed October 7, 2024.

Page 24, "I feel like basketball . . ." Andrea Adelson, "Caitlin Clark's Record Year of Basketball Ends in Playoff Sweep," espn.com, September 26, 2024, https://www.espn.com/wnba/story/_/id/41447804/indiana-fever-star-caitlin-clark-record-year-basketball-ends-playoff-sweep, Accessed October 7, 2024.

Any additional websites and resources referenced in this book are not maintained, authorized, or sponsored by Capstone. All product and company names are trademarks™ or registered® trademarks of their respective holders.

TABLE OF CONTENTS

WELCOME TO THE WNBA..................... 4

CHAPTER ONE
HIGH SCHOOL HOOP STAR 6

CHAPTER TWO
HOMETOWN HAWKEYE 10

CHAPTER THREE
ROOKIE SENSATION 18

CHAPTER FOUR
FIRST PLAYOFFS 22

CHAPTER FIVE
BIGGER THAN BASKETBALL 26

TIMELINE...............................29
GLOSSARY.............................30
READ MORE 31
INTERNET SITES 31
INDEX 32

Words in **BOLD** are in the glossary.

WELCOME TO THE WNBA

Indiana Fever **rookie** Caitlin Clark stole the ball and raced up the court. It was her Women's National Basketball Association (WNBA) **debut**. The Fever were playing a road game against the Connecticut Sun. Clark wove through the Sun's defense. She laid the ball off the glass. It was her first professional basket. The sold-out crowd erupted in cheers!

Clark was the most **anticipated** rookie in WNBA history. Minutes later, she took a pass at the top of the arc and buried a three-pointer. Again, the crowd went wild. Clark finished with 20 points.

The Sun defeated Clark and the Fever 92–71. Still, Clark's debut was the first sellout in Connecticut in 20 years. The game drew more than 2.1 million viewers on television.

FACT

Clark was being **recruited** by colleges before she played a single high school game.

CHAPTER ONE
HIGH SCHOOL HOOP STAR

Caitlin Elizabeth Clark was born January 22, 2002, in Des Moines, Iowa. She has an older brother, Blake, and a younger brother, Colin. Her parents, Brent and Anne Clark, say she was a **competitor** from an early age. Clark began playing organized basketball when she was 5. Her dad coached her first team. She often played against boys who were older and bigger.

Clark began playing **Amateur** Athletic Union (AAU) basketball at age 7. Her dad couldn't find a girls' league for players that young. So again, Clark played on a boys' team. She helped the team win the AAU Iowa state tournament. Clark was so talented that a parent from another team complained it wasn't fair for her to play on the boys' AAU team.

>>> Clark holding the 2024 AP Player of the Year award and posing with her parents

Soccer Star

Clark was a superstar on the soccer pitch as well. She scored 23 goals in just 13 games as a freshman. She quit soccer after her sophomore season to focus on basketball. Experts say her soccer skills are what make her such a great passer on the basketball court.

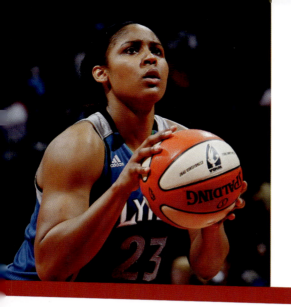

Full Circle Moment

Growing up, Minnesota Lynx player Maya Moore was one of Clark's idols. Clark went to lots of Lynx games with her dad. In 2024, Clark was playing in Minnesota the night that Moore's number was retired.

Clark attended Dowling Catholic High School in West Des Moines. Most freshmen begin their high school careers on the bench. Not Clark. She stepped onto the court during her first game as a starting point guard. She held this position for the next four seasons.

The highlights were endless. In one game, Clark scored 60 points. That included a school record of 13 three-point shots! She was the leading scorer in Iowa her junior year. Her senior year, Clark led the state in scoring for the second season in a row. She was named a McDonald's All-American and the 2020 Miss Iowa Basketball.

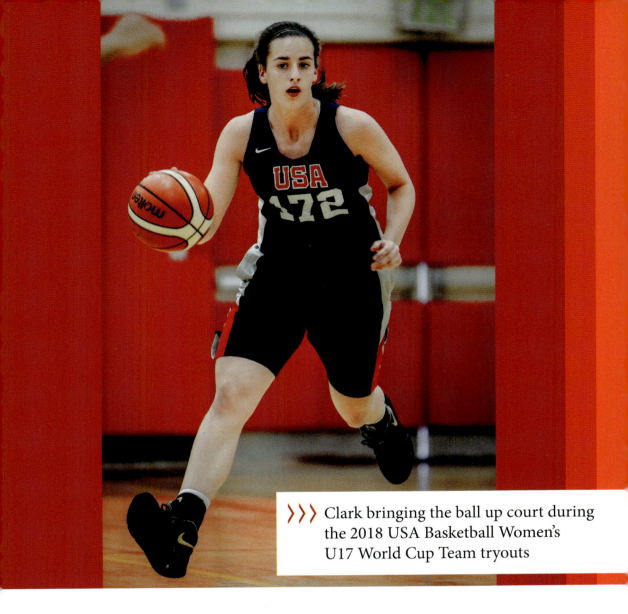

>>> Clark bringing the ball up court during the 2018 USA Basketball Women's U17 World Cup Team tryouts

Clark was one of the most **dominant** players in high school basketball. But not everything was perfect for Clark. In 2017, she made USA's U16 National Team. However, she did not make the U17 team the next year. It was a surprise. She used that to motivate her to work even harder.

CHAPTER TWO
HOMETOWN HAWKEYE

By graduation, Clark had been receiving college offers for years. All the basketball powerhouses wanted her. They included Notre Dame, Iowa, Texas, Louisville, Oregon State, and Missouri. Clark had a tough choice to make. In the end, she decided to stay close to home. She became a Hawkeye at the University of Iowa.

FACT

At Iowa, Clark chose uniform number 22 to match her birthday of January 22.

"I think playing for your home state is always special," Clark said after selecting Iowa. She let Hawkeye fans know she had big dreams for her home state team. "I have goals for a Final Four. Who wouldn't want to win and be the best?"

On November 25, 2020, Clark stepped onto Iowa's home court. She didn't play like an 18-year-old in her first college game. She led her team to a solid 96–81 win. Clark's debut numbers were impressive. She finished the game with 27 points, eight rebounds, and four assists.

And Clark didn't slow down. She scored more than 30 points in 12 out of the 30 games. She started in each game and averaged 26.6 points per game.

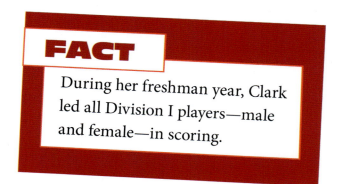

FACT

During her freshman year, Clark led all Division I players—male and female—in scoring.

››› Clark fighting for a shot against two Central Michigan defenders

During her junior year, Clark led the Hawkeyes to the national championship game for the first time in the program's history. But the Hawkeyes were outplayed by future WNBA star Angel Reese and LSU. Iowa lost 102–85.

>>> Clark (left), Reese (middle), and Gabbie Marshall fight for position under the basket.

By the end of her senior year, Clark was the NCAA all-time scoring leader. She led the NCAA in three-pointers per game, career assists, free throws made, and field goals made. Could she end her college career with a national championship?

In April 2024, Clark led the Hawkeyes back to the NCAA Championship game. Iowa squared off against the undefeated South Carolina Gamecocks. Despite Clark leading the team with 30 points, it wasn't enough. The Gamecocks ended Clark's dream with an 87–75 win.

>>> Raven Johnson (number 25) tried to stop Clark during the championship game.

After the game, Clark displayed the positive attitude that has earned her the respect of millions of fans worldwide.

"I'm sad we lost this game," she said. "But I'm also so proud of myself and my teammates and this program."

Clark's final college game set a viewing record. As many as 24 million people watched the game live on television. It was the first time the women's NCAA final drew a larger audience than the men's.

Scoring Champ

In more than 130 years, no college basketball player has scored more points than Clark. On March 3, 2024, she stepped to the free throw line in the second quarter. She was tied with "Pistol" Pete Maravich at 3,667 career points. Clark knocked down the free throw, and the crowd burst into cheers. Clark finished her college career with 3,951 points.

CHAPTER THREE
ROOKIE SENSATION

The Indiana Fever picked Clark first in the 2024 WNBA **draft**. She entered the league with high expectations and lots of pressure. Teams hosting the Fever moved games to larger arenas to meet the demand for tickets. And even the larger arenas would sell out!

››› Clark scoring her first WNBA basket

On May 14, 2024, Clark played her first WNBA game. The Fever lost to the Connecticut Sun. Clark scored 20 points. She also had 10 turnovers. Ten days later, Clark posted her first double-double with 11 points, 10 rebounds, and eight assists. The Fever beat the Los Angeles Sparks 78–73.

Endorsements vs. Salary

Clark signed a $28 million **endorsement** deal with Nike before she played a single WNBA game. The Nike deal will earn Clark more than she is expected to earn playing basketball during her entire WNBA career. Clark's salary for her rookie season was $76,000.

>>> Clark shooting over a Lynx player

On August 24, 2024, the Fever were in Minnesota to take on the Lynx. It was just 29 games into Clark's professional career, and she was about to set a WNBA record. The Fever trailed by nine as Clark advanced the ball up court.

The rookie began to drive to the basket before pulling up and hitting an easy shot. The bucket made Clark the youngest player and the only rookie in WNBA history to score 500 points.

Clark finished the 2024 regular season with an incredible 769 points. She set rookie records for assists and three-pointers. Clark earned 66 of 67 first-place votes to be named Rookie of the Year.

>>> Clark holding the Rookie of the Year award

CHAPTER FOUR
FIRST PLAYOFFS

The Fever started the 2024 season 1–8. They finished the season with a record of 20–20. This was a big improvement from their 13–27 record from the year before. Even better, it earned them a spot in the playoffs for the first time since 2016.

Game 1 against the Connecticut Sun did not go well for the Fever. Clark was poked in the right eye in the first quarter. She didn't miss any time, but it was a tough way to start the game. The Fever lost by 24 points. Clark ended the game with 11 points, eight assists, three steals, and two turnovers.

FACT

The Fever sold more tickets than any other team in the WNBA. Jersey sales, TV ratings, and attendance all reached record highs in 2024 as fans came out to support Clark.

>>> Getting a good look at the basket, Clark took a shot from beyond the three-point line.

23

In Game 2, Clark played all 40 minutes. She put up 25 points with six rebounds and nine assists. She was aggressive on defense. But it wasn't enough. The Sun harassed Clark all night. She finished 3–12 from three-point range. The Fever kept the game close. Still, the Sun held on for an 87–81 win and the series sweep.

"It's a good little taste of what's possible for this organization and for this franchise," Clark said after the game.

During her first year in the WNBA, Clark dominated offensively. She led the league in assists. She finished seventh in points scored. She finished first in three-point shooting. However, she also led the WNBA in turnovers. And after years in the spotlight, Clark was looking forward to a few weeks off.

"I feel like basketball has really consumed my life for a year. So I feel like it'll be good for me to kind of reflect back on everything that's happened," she said at the end of the season.

CHAPTER FIVE
BIGGER THAN BASKETBALL

Clark has had a huge impact on the WNBA. Media members call it the "Caitlin Clark Effect." It began the night Clark was drafted by the Indiana Fever. The televised draft drew four times more viewers than in 2023. ESPN ranked Clark the fourth most popular athlete in America in 2024. As a rookie, Clark had the top-selling jersey in the WNBA.

Clark serves as a role model for millions of young women both on and off the court. She gives back by teaching the game to children at her annual basketball skills camp. She started the Caitlin Clark Foundation to help young people through education, nutrition, and sports. Clark has also volunteered for Habitat for Humanity. This organization builds affordable housing.

If her career ended today, Caitlin Clark would be remembered as one of the greatest college basketball players of all time. But Clark is hoping for a long career in the WNBA. She wants to win championships. She wants to dominate.

Time will tell if Clark has what it takes to be an all-time great. Her fans believe she will. One thing is for sure. It took Clark only one season in the WNBA to change the game of women's basketball forever.

TIMELINE

2002 — Born on January 22 in Des Moines, Iowa

2017 — Wins first gold medal as a member of the U.S. Women's team in the FIBA Under-16 Americas Championship

2020 — Accepts offer to play Division I basketball for the Iowa Hawkeyes

2021 — Named MVP of the FIBA Under-19 World Cup, winning her third gold medal

2024 — Sets the all-time NCAA scoring record, finishing the season with 3,951 points

2024 — Selected as the first pick in the WNBA draft by the Indiana Fever

2024 — Signs a $28 million endorsement deal with Nike that includes her own shoe

2024 — Sets WNBA single-season record with 322 assists

2024 — Named WNBA Rookie of the Year

GLOSSARY

AMATEUR (AH-muh-chuhr)—describing a sports league where athletes compete for fun and are not paid

ANTICIPATE (an-TIH-suh-payt)—to look forward to something

COMPETITOR (kuhm-PEH-tuh-tuhr)—person trying to win a sport or game

DEBUT (DAY-byoo)—player's first game

DOMINANT (DAH-muh-nuhnt)—powerful or important

DRAFT (DRAFT)—process of selecting new players to join a professional sports team

ENDORSEMENT (in-DOR-smuhnt)—act of wearing, promoting, or using a product in exchange for money

RECRUIT (ri-KROOT)—to ask someone to join a team or organization

ROOKIE (RUH-kee)—first-year player in a professional sports league

READ MORE

Borzilleri, Meri-Jo. *Who Is Caitlin Clark?* New York: Penguin Workshop, 2025.

Chandler, Matt. *Basketball's Origin Story.* North Mankato, MN: Capstone Press, 2025.

Sports Illustrated Kids. *Big Book of WHO: Women in Sports.* New York: Sports Illustrated, 2024.

INTERNET SITES

Caitlin Clark Foundation
caitlinclark22.com

Kiddle: Caitlin Clark Facts for Kids
kids.kiddle.co/Caitlin_Clark

Kiddle: WNBA Facts for Kids
kids.kiddle.co/Women%27s_National_Basketball_Association

WNBA History
wnba.com/history

INDEX

2020 Miss Iowa Basketball, 8

AAU basketball, 6

"Caitlin Clark Effect," 26

college offers, 5, 10

endorsements, 19

family, 6, 7, 8
final college game, 16
first college game, 12
first high school game, 8
first WNBA game, 4, 19

giving back, 27

high school, 8, 9
hometown, 6

Indiana Fever, 4, 18, 19, 20, 22, 24

McDonald's All-American, 8

NCAA National Championship Game, 14, 15

Rookie of the Year, 21

scoring records, 8, 12, 17
soccer, 7

University of Iowa, 10, 11, 12, 14, 15
USA basketball, 9

WNBA draft, 18
WNBA playoffs, 22, 24
WNBA records, 20–21

AUTHOR BIO

Matt Chandler is the author of more than 60 books for children and thousands of articles published in newspapers and magazines. He writes mostly nonfiction books with a focus on sports, ghosts and haunted places, and graphic novels. Matt lives in New York.